WELCOME TO THE ULTI CRICKET QUIZ BOOK

The questions and answers are accurate as of September 2021

Paragon Publishing offers a wide range of other sports themed quizzes, books and crosswords if you have enjoyed this one

CONTENTS

WORLD CUP/ ODI WORLD CUP

1. When was the first Cricket World Cup held?
a. 1968 b. 1970 c. 1973 d. 1975

2. Which country hosted the first ever ODI World Cup?

3. Which country won the first ever Cricket World Cup?

4. How often is the Cricket World Cup held?

5. Which country has won the most World Cup titles?

6. Which batsman has scored the greatest number of runs in World Cup history?

7. Which bowler has taken the greatest number of wickets in the tournament's history?

8. Which country won the 2019 World Cup?

9. In the 2015 World Cup final, who started New Zealand's downfall which saw them lose their last seven wickets for only 33 runs?

10. In the 1996 World Cup final, only one bowler ended up picking multiple wickets. Who was it?
a. Sanath Jayasurya b. Muttiah Muralitharan
c. Chaminda Vaas   d. Aravinda De Silva

11. Which country won the 1979 World Cup final?

12. Which country is set to host the 2023 World Cup?

13. Which of the following years holds the record for the most maidens in a World Cup final?
a. 1975 b. 1979 c. 1983 d. 1987

14. Kapil Dev's memorable running catch to dismiss Sir Viv Richards in the 1983 World Cup final is known to all. Who was the bowler in that dismissal?
a. Mohinder Amarnath   b. Balwinder Sandhu
c. Roger Binny   d. Madan Lal

15. Which bowler holds the unwanted record for the most expensive figures in a World Cup final?
a. Dilhara Fernando   b. Trent Boult
c. Nuwan Kulasekara   d. Javagal Srinath

16. Chris Woakes recently revealed it all about England's late tactical change in their third-choice batsman for the Super Over in the 2019 WC final. Who did they bring in?
a. Eoin Morgan   b. Jason Roy
c. Jonny Bairstow   d. Joe Root

17. Who, among the following pairs, did not bowl their full quota of overs in the 2011 World Cup final?
a. Munaf Patel-Harbhajan Singh
b. Sreesanth-Yuvraj Singh
c. Munaf Patel-Sreesanth
d. Harbhajan Singh-Yuvraj Singh

18. What is the largest margin by which a country has won the World Cup final?
a. 105 runs   b. 125 runs   c. 145 runs

19. What is the largest margin by which a country has won a World Cup match?
a. 215 runs   b. 255 runs   c. 275 runs

20. When was the last time the West Indies played in the World Cup final?
a. 1983   b. 1985   c. 1987   d. 1989

21. When did India win its first World Cup?
a. 1976   b. 1979   c. 1983   d. 1985

22. When was the first ever Man of the Tournament title awarded in the World Cup?
a. 1988   b. 1990   c. 1992   d. 1994

23. Which player was declared Man of the Tournament in the 2019 World Cup?

24. Which player won the Man of the Match in the 2011 World Cup final?

25. Who was the Man of the Match in the 2019 World Cup final?

26. What is the highest number of runs scored by a player in a World Cup match?
a. 209   b. 237   c. 249   d. 287

27. Which batsman has taken the greatest number of runs in a single World Cup?

28. Which bowler has taken the most wickets in a single tournament?

29. Which player has taken the greatest number of catches in the World Cup?

30. Which wicket keeper holds the record of most dismissals in World Cup history?

31. In which year did India and Pakistan jointly host the World Cup?

32. Which two players have the record of the highest partnership by runs?
a. SC Ganguly, R Dravid
b. WU Tharanga, TM Dilshan
c. CH Gayle, MN Samuels
d. DA Warner, SPD Smith

33. What is the second highest partnership by runs in the history of the World Cup?
a. 285   b. 318   c. 341   d. 378

34. As of September 2021, how many times have Australia appeared in the World Cup final?
a. 7   b. 8   c. 9   d. 10

35. What is the largest margin by which a country has won the World Cup final?
a. 5 wickets   b. 6 wickets
c. 7 wickets   d. 8 wickets

36. Ricky Ponting has scored the second greatest number of runs in the history of the World Cup. How many runs has he scored?
a. 1532   b. 1743   c. 1875   d. 2019

37. What is the highest number of runs Chris Gayle scored in a World Cup match?
a. 182   b. 198   c. 215   d. 229

38. Which batsman scored the most runs in the 1999 World Cup?

39. Which two bowlers took the most wickets at the 1999 World Cup?
a. Geoff Allott   b. Glenn McGrath
c. Lance Klusener   d. Shane Warne

40. Who was the leading run scorer in the 1996 Cricket World Cup?

41. Who took the most wickets in the 1996 tournament?
a. Waqar Younis   b. Anil Kumble
c. Paul Strang   d. Roger Harper

42. Which of these teams have never won the men's World Cup?
a. Pakistan   b. South Africa   c. Sri Lanka

43. Who has played the most matches as captain in men's World Cups?

44. Who was the first captain to lift the World Cup trophy?

45. Of the first seven World Cups, 1975 to 1999, which city hosted the most finals?

46. Who was Holland's leading run getter in the 1996 World Cup?

47. The first matches of the first World Cup took place on June 7, 1975. On this day, which batsman scored 171 not out?

48. In total, how many nations played in the first eight World Cups?
a. 13   b. 15   c. 17   d. 19

49. Which nation lost the most games in the first eight World Cups?
a. South Africa   b. Sri Lanka   c. Zimbabwe

50. Against which country did Bangladesh produce an upset victory in the 1999 World Cup?

ICC WORLD TEST CHAMPIONSHIP

1. Who is the highest run-scorer in ICC World Test Championship history?

2. Who is the leading wicket-taker in ICC World Test Championship history?

3. Who registered the best bowling figures in an innings in the ICC World Test Championship?

4. Which wicket-keeper has affected the most dismissals in the ICC World Test Championship?

5. Which pair had the highest partnership by runs in the ICC World Test Championship?

6. Name the bowler who picked up the first wicket in the ICC World Test Championship.

7. Who effected the most dismissals in an innings in the World Test Championship?

8. Who has the most hundreds in the ICC World Test Championship?

9. Which bowler has the most five-wicket hauls in the ICC World Test Championship?

10. Which team registered the highest total in the ICC World Test Championship?

11. What is the highest number of runs scored in a Test Championship match?
a. 265   b. 295   c. 315   d. 335

12. What is the highest number of runs scored by Virat Kohli in a Test Championship match?
a. 254   b. 265   c. 282   d. 300

13. How many runs has Virat Kohli scored in the World Test Championship tournament?
a. 1024   b. 1152   c. 1321   d. 1485

14. Two players are tied for the most sixes in the World Test Championship tournament. Can you name both players?

15. Which player has taken the most catches in the World Test Championship?

16. Known for his fielding, how many catches has Virat Kohli taken in the tournament?
a. 24   b. 30   c. 36   d. 42

17. Which country has won the World Test championship match by the largest margin(runs)?

IPL

1. Who is the leading run scorer in the IPL?

2. Amit Mishra is the second leading wicket taker in the IPL. How many wickets has he taken?
a. 152   b. 166   c. 180   d. 195

3. Which wicket keeper holds the record of most dismissals in the IPL?

4. KD Karthik is one of the leading wicket keepers in the history of IPL. How many dismissals does he have to his name?
a. 105   b. 128   c. 144   d. 179

5. Which umpire has umpired for the greatest number of matches in the history of IPL?

6. Which batsman is the Mumbai Indians' leading run scorer?

7. Which bowler is the Mumbai Indians'
leading wicket taker?

8. What is the highest number of runs scored
by the Mumbai Indians in an IPL match?
a. 223   b. 254   c. 273   d. 296

9. How many times have the Rajasthan Royals
won the IPL?

10. When did the Kolkata Knight Riders first
win the IPL?
a. 2006   b. 2008   c. 2010   d. 2012

11. When did the Mumbai Indians first win the
IPL?
a. 2005   b. 2009   c. 2013   d. 2015

12. Who is the Kolkata Knight Riders' leading
run scorer?

13. Who is the leading wicket taker for the
Kolkata Knight Riders?

14. Who was the captain of the Mumbai Indians in IPL 2012?

15. Which team picked up Australia all-rounder Marnus Labuschagne during the mini auction ahead of IPL 2021?

16. Which Indian player has scored the fastest hundred in the IPL?

17. Which two teams made their IPL debuts in 2011?

18. Who was the first cricketer to be sold at the IPL 2021 auction?

19. Who was the first overseas player to captain Delhi Daredevils (now Delhi Capitals)?

20. Which venue hosted the IPL 2014 final?

21. Who is the only bowler to have picked up a five-wicket haul twice against the same team in the same season of the IPL?

22. Who has the highest all-time batting average (having featured in a minimum of 10 matches)?

23. Which player has won the greatest number of IPL orange caps, which are awarded to the season's highest run-scorer?

24. Which batsman has scored the greatest number of hundreds in the IPL?

25. Who has the best all-time bowling average in the IPL?

26. Which team has played in the most IPL finals after Chennai Super Kings?

27. In the 2014 edition of the IPL, a part of the tournament was held in the UAE. Which batsman was the top scorer?

28. How many IPL finals has Mahendra Singh Dhoni played in?
a. 5   b. 7   c. 8   d. 10

29. What is the approximate value of the IPL brand?

a. $1.2 billion   c. $2.8 billion   d. $4.1 billion

30. Where was the first IPL match played in India?

31. Which country hosted the IPL's second edition?

32. Which team won the IPL tournament in 2009?

33. Which IPL team does Shah Rukh Khan own?

34. In which year was the first IPL tournament held?

35. What is the minimum number of players needed in a squad?

a. 15   b. 16   c. 17   d. 18

36. What is the minimum number of Indian players needed in a squad?
a. 8   b. 10   c. 12   d. 14

37. How many Indians have won the MVP award?
a. 2   b. 3   c. 4   d. 5

38. Which player has the most wickets (119) in the history of IPL?

39. Who was the first Indian captain to hold the IPL trophy?

40. Which of these IPL franchises was banned for two years?
a. Chennai Super Kings   b. Gujarat Lions
c. Pune Supergiants

41. Who was the second captain to lift the IPL trophy?
a. Gautam Gambhir   b. Adam Gilchrist
c. Mahendra Singh Dhoni   d. David Warner

42. Which IPL franchise has Indian cricketer Yuvraj Singh never played for?
a. Bangalore   b. Kolkata   c. Hyderabad

43. Who was the first batsman to score a century in the IPL?

44. Which of these cricketers has been playing for the same franchise for their entire career?
a. M.S. Dhoni   b. Ravindra Jadeja
c. Virat Kohli

45. True or false: Punjab Kings and Rajasthan Royals have played each other 4 times in the season opener.

46. Who took the first hat-trick in an IPL match?

47. How many hat-tricks did Yuvraj Singh take in his IPL career?
a. 2   b. 3   c. 4   d. 5

48. How many teams have won two or more IPL trophies?

49. Which batsman scored the most runs in the first ever game of the IPL?
a. Gautam Gambhir   b. Sanath Jayasuriya
c. Shaun Marsh

50. Who was the first bowler to pick up a six-four in an IPL match?

51. Who was the first Indian to slam a century in the IPL?

52. Which captain has won the most IPL titles?

53. Where was the first IPL century hit?
a. Mumbai   b. Kolkata   c. Bangalore

54. Which city is the second home for IPL franchise Chennai Super Kings?
a. Bangalore   b. Mumbai   c. Delhi

55. Who was the coach of Rajasthan Royals when they lifted the maiden IPL trophy?

56. Which team was the winner of IPL 2011?

57. Who was the coach of Chennai Super King in IPL 2010?
a. Mike Hussey   b. Stephen Fleming
c. Kepler Wessels

58. Which IPL franchise did AB De Villiers play for before being inducted into RCB?

59. Which of these players has not registered a hattrick in an IPL match?
a. Rohit Sharma   b. Yuvraj Singh
c. RP Singh

60. What is the individual highest score in IPL history?
a. 135   b. 153   c. 175   d. 204

61. When did MS Dhoni first lift the IPL trophy?
a. 2008   b. 2010   c. 2011   d. 2014

62. Who was the purple cap winner in IPL season 2015?

63. Which of the following players has been captain of Gujarat Lions?
a. Suresh Raina   b. Ravindra Jadeja
c. R Ashwin

64. Who was the captain of Kings XI Punjab team in 2009?

65. How many centuries has Sachin Tendulkar hit in his IPL career?
a. 1   b. 2   c. 3   d. 5

66. Who bowled the final ball in IPL season 11?
a. Lasith Malinga   b. Jaspreet Bumrah
c. Ravindra Jadega

67. How many teams has Mahendra Singh Dhoni represented in the IPL?
a. 1   b. 2   c. 3   d. 4

68. Which bowler bowled the first ever ball in IPL history?
a. Sohail Tanvir   b. Praveen Kumar
c. Zaheer Khan

69. Who scored the first century in the 2013 IPL season?
a. Virat Kohli   b. Suresh Raina
c. Rohit Sharma

70. Name the wicketkeeper who effected the greatest number of dismissals until IPL 2018.
a. Dinesh Karthik   b. Adam Gilchrist
c. Mahendra Singh Dhoni

71. How many balls did Brendon McCullum face enroute to his maiden ton in IPL?
a. 67   b. 73   c. 79   d. 86

72. Who has slammed 4 or more centuries in the same IPL season?

73. Where was the final match of IPL 2017 played?
a. Mumbai   b. Hyderabad   c. Chennai

74. Who took the first wicket of IPL 2019?
a. Deepak Chahar   b. Harbhajan Singh
c. Dwayne Bravo

75. Who was the first player to score 4,000 runs in the IPL?
a. Chris Gayle   b. Suresh Raina
c. Virat Kohli

SACHIN TENDULKAR

1. Tendulkar scored a hundred in his first match as India captain. Who were his opponents?
a. Sri Lanka   b. Australia
c. Zimbabwe   d. Pakistan

2. Against which country did Sachin Tendulkar score 200 runs in an ODI match?

3. Tendulkar claimed his first ODI five-wicket haul in Kochi. Where did he get his second five-wicket haul?

4. Who was Tendulkar's first wicket in international cricket?
a. Aashish Kapoor   b. Anil Kumble
c. Roshan Mahanama

5. Who, among the following, has not captained Tendulkar in international cricket?
a. Kapil Dev   b. Mahendra Singh Dhoni
c. Sourav Ganguly

6. Tendulkar has dismissed this batsman eight times in international matches. He hasn't dismissed anyone else more than four times. Who is this batsman?

7. In the 73 ODIs where Tendulkar captained India, there was only one draw. Who were the opponents?

8. Who was Tendulkar's single wicket in his solitary T20 international?

9. Which batsman has been out via a catch nine times by Tendulkar in all internationals?
a. Shahid Afridi   b. Sean Abbott
c. Anwar Hossain   d. Rober Croft

10. Who is the only cricketer to have been out by hit-wicket to Tendulkar in an international match?

11. Name the only team that India beat more than once in Tests when Tendulkar was captain.
a. Australia   b. England   c. South Africa

12. In the 1991-92 Benson & Hedges series, Tendulkar took the last West Indian wicket in a Perth ODI to force a tie as India defended 126. Which batsman did he dismiss?

13. How many ODI series outside India did the team win under Tendulkar's captaincy?
a. 0   b. 1   c. 2   d. 3

14. In all the IPL seasons he has played in, Tendulkar has bowled in only one season. Which one?
a. 2008   b. 2009   c. 2010   d. 2011

15. Tendulkar's best contribution to his first Test in England was a catch he took at long-on. Which batsman did he dismiss?

THE ASHES

1. Which two countries are The Ashes played between?

2. Which format of cricket is played in The Ashes?

3. When was The Ashes first played?
a. 1882   b. 1889   c. 1897   d. 1901

4. How many matches are traditionally played in The Ashes?

5. How many Ashes series have been played?
a. 61   b. 71   c. 86   d. 108

6. How many Ashes series have Australia won?
a. 26   b. 33   c. 38   d. 45

7. How many Ashes series have England won?
a. 25   b. 32   c. 36   d. 41

8. How many Ashes series have been a draw?
a. 5   b. 6   c. 7   d. 8

9. Which batsman has scored the most runs in The Ashes?

10. Which bowler has taken the most wickets in The Ashes?

11. England holds the bragging rights for winning a Test match in 1938 with the biggest margin of runs ever seen at The Ashes. How big was it?
a. 374   b. 453   c. 579   d. 672

12. Australia won by their biggest margin of runs in Brisbane in 1946, but how big was it?
a. 332   b. 389   c. 458   d. 498

13. In which year did an Australian team first tour the UK?
a. 1868   b. 1874   c. 1979   d. 1983

14. How often do The Ashes take place?

15. What number Ashes was the 2010 Ashes?
a. 65th   b. 66th   c. 67th   d. 68th

16. When did the women's Test series between Australia and England officially become the Women's Ashes?
a. 1996   b. 1998   c. 2000   d. 2002

17. In which year did England captain, Joe Root, become the youngest England player to score a century in an Ashes match?
a. 2012   b. 2013   c. 2014   d. 2015

18. Who was the only Englishman to score a century in the 2013-14 series?

19. Who is the only batsman in the past 25 years to have twice scored three centuries in a single Ashes series?

20. Who was Australia's leading run-scorer in the 2013 series?

21. Name the batsman who was the top scorer for Australia in the first innings of the opening match of the 2013 series.

22. How many Ashes hundreds has Australia captain Michael Clarke made?
a. 5   b. 7   c. 9

23. Who won more Ashes series: Steve Waugh or Shane Warne?

24. Who took the most wickets for Australia in the second innings of the final Test at The Oval in 2009?

25. Mitchell Johnson took 37 wickets in the 2013-14 Ashes, but how many has he taken in England?
a. 18   b. 23   c. 28   d. 34

26. How many Ashes Tests did Steve Smith take to score his first hundred?
a. 2   b. 4   c. 6   d. 8

27. Who is the only person to have taken a hat-trick and made a half-century in an Ashes Test?

28. Who is the only man to play Test cricket for England against Australia and for Australia against England?

29. Who played Ashes cricket for Australia but never played first-class cricket in Australia?

30. Which bowler once took five wickets in seven balls in Ashes cricket?

31. Name the only Ashes player to have all the letters of the word 'Cricket' in his surname.

32. How many runs did Graeme Swann concede in the final over of his Test career?
a. 19   b. 22   c. 24   d. 27

33. Who umpired an Ashes Test before playing one?

34. Who is the only man to play in all five Tests in an Ashes series and not be dismissed?

35. What is the greatest number of runs from one stroke in Ashes history?

36. What was the name given to the Australian team that toured England in 1948?

37. In which country was the Ashes held in 2006?

38. True or false: the 2006 Ashes was a 5-0 score line.

39. Which young Australian batsman scored an impressive 839 runs in the 1989 Ashes series?

40. Having spent the majority of the 1980s injured, which bowler came back to England and delivered 41 wickets on the 1989 Ashes tour?

41. Before the tour, Steve Waugh was yet to score a century in Test cricket. At the end of the tour, he had achieved 506 runs with an average of 126.5. How many Test centuries had he scored by the end of the 1989 Ashes series?

42. Which Australian leg spinner, that was born in 1954, played seven career Test matches for Australia?

43. One of the rare positives for the English team in the 1989 Ashes series was that a player scored 553 runs with an average of 61.4. Which player was this?

44. England's captain started the 1989 series badly by sending the Australians in to bat in the first Test, which resulted in the press calling for him to be axed. The captain responded with a century in the second Test and managed to stay in control for the rest of the series. Who was this English captain?

45. During the 1989 series England used 28 players while Australia used 12 including one surprise pick for the first test. A young fast bowler from Tasmania. What was his name?

46. What was the final score for the 1989 series?

47. What did the first Test match in 1876/77 have in common with the centenary Test match that was played one hundred years later?

48. Name the first batsman to achieve a century in England vs Australia Test matches?

49. Which English all-rounder was the backbone for the "Miracle at Headingly" in 1981 with his undefeated innings of 149?

50. When Jim Laker had match figures of 19/90 at Old Trafford in 1956, who took the other Australian wicket?

51. Which Australian tour party provided all five of Wisden's Cricketers of the Year for the only time in the 20th Century?

52. Which Test cricket ground had its first day of Test cricket completely washed out in 1884?

53. What name was given to the heated Test series that was played in the 1932-33 Ashes in Australia when Douglas Jardine led England to a 4-1 series victory?

54. On June 4, 1993, English batsman Mike Gatting had just been bowled by the supposed "Ball of the Century". Who was the bowler?

55. Name the pair of bowlers that destroyed the England team at the 1974-75 Ashes.

56. Which English off-spinner had a near perfect Test match when he took nineteen of the possible twenty wickets against Australia in Manchester in 1956?

57. Gary Pratt's run out of Ricky Ponting in 2005 at Trent Bridge brought about some questionable words from the Australian captain. What was Pratt's position in the England team?

58. Which Australian batsman announced himself to the scene in his debut Test match in 1977 when he hit five consecutive boundaries off England's Tony Greig?

59. Which Australian was only two runs short of completing the first ever century by a number eleven batsman in a Test match in 2013?

60. Needing only four runs in his last Test innings to finish with a career average of 100, Donald Bradman was dismissed for a duck by Eric Hollies. What sort of bowler was Hollies?

ICC CHAMPIONS TROPHY

1. Which year was the first Champions Trophy tournament played?
a. 1994   b. 1996   c. 1998   d. 2000

2. Which country hosted the first Champions Trophy tournament?
a. England   b. India   c. Bangladesh

3. Which cricket format is played in the Champions Trophy tournament?

4. Which country won the first ever Champions Trophy tournament?
a. Pakistan   b. West Indies
c. New Zealand   d. South Africa

5. How many countries have won the Champions Trophy twice?

6. Which of these countries have won the Champions Trophy more than once?
a. Pakistan   b. Australia
c. Sri Lanka   d. India

7. Which country won the Champions Tournament in 2013?

8. Which country hosted the tournament when Australia won the trophy in 2006?

9. Which batsman has scored the most runs in the tournament?

10. Which bowler has taken the most wickets in the Champions Trophy?

11. Which country was the winner of the 2017 Champions Trophy?

12. Which two countries were declared co-champions in the year 2002?

13. How many countries have entered the tournament final three times?
a. 1   b. 2   c. 3   d. 4

14. Which country or countries have played in the final three or more times?

15. Following the 2017 Champions Trophy, when is the next Champions Trophy scheduled to be held?

16. Which team won the first-ever match in the history of the ICC Champions Trophy?
a. South Africa   b. Australia
c. New Zealand   d. West Indies

17. Which two teams contested the finals of the first ICC Champions Trophy in Dhaka?

18. Which team was the first to score over 300 in an innings in the ICC Champions Trophy?
a. Pakistan   b. Sri Lanka   c. India

19. South Africa has also scored 300 in an innings in the ICC Champions Trophy. Against which team did they post this huge total?

20. Which team has the unfortunate record of being the first to be bowled out for less than a 100 in the competition?
a. Bangladesh   b. Sri Lanka   c. India

21. England have generally had a bad run of form in this tournament, winning only two matches in the first 3 tournaments (against Bangladesh and Zimbabwe). Who was the first Englishman to score a century in this tournament?

22. Which "non-cricketing" country was a shock entry to the 2004 tournament?

23. Other than Australia, which other team went winless in the 2017 tournament?

24. Pakistan were 162/7 chasing a target of 237 against Sri Lanka in a do-or-die match in the 2017 Champions Trophy tournament. Who partnered captain Sarfaraz Ahmed to take Pakistan to the win from that position with a score of 75?

25. Which losing team succumbed to the highest successful run-chase in competition history in 2017?
a. Pakistan   b. England
c. India   d. Zimbabwe

26. Name the only bowler to take a 5-wicket haul in the 2017 tournament.

27. Who was the only player in the tournament to have played his sixth consecutive ICC Champions Trophy in 2017?

28. Hardik Pandya hit a hat-trick of sixes twice during the Champions Trophy in 2017. Shadab Khan was one bowler, who was the other?

ICC T20 WORLD CUP

1. When was the first T20 World Cup held?
a. 2004   b. 2005   c. 2006   d. 2007

2. Which batsman has scored the most runs in the tournament?

3. Which bowler has taken the most wickets in the tournament?

4. Which country first hosted the T20 World Cup?
a. England   b. Bangladesh   c. South Africa

5. Which two countries entered the final of the first ever T20 World Cup?
a. West Indies   b. England
c. India   d. Pakistan

6. How many countries have won the tournament more than once?

7. Which country or countries have won the tournament more than once?

8. Which country hosted the T20 World Cup in 2016?

9. Which country won the 2016 T20 World Championships?

10. Which is the only country to appear in the T20 World Cup final three times?

11. Following the 2016 T20 World Cup, when is the next T20 World Cup set to be held?

12. This wicket-keeper made the most dismissals in the 2007 T20 World Cup.

13. Who dismissed Yuvraj Singh in the game against England after he hit six sixes off Stuart Broad in 2007?

14. In the 2007 final between Pakistan and India, there were three fast bowlers who took three-wicket hauls. Two were Irfan Pathan and RP Singh. Who was the third?

15. South Africa chased down 206 in the 2007 tournament opener against West Indies. Who was their top scorer?

16. Who hit the most sixes in the tournament in 2007?

17. Which New Zealand bowler recorded the best figures in the 2007 T20 World Cup?

18. Which player has hit the most sixes in an innings in the T20 World Cup Tournament?

19. Which bowler has taken the most wickets in an innings in the tournament?

20. What's the highest number of runs scored in a T20 World Cup match by a batsman?
a. 123   b. 138   c. 152   d. 174

21. What is the highest number of runs scored by Chris Gayle in a T20 World Cup match?
a. 99   b. 106   c. 117   d. 129

22. Which player has taken most catches in the T20 World Cup tournament?

23. Which player has played the highest number of matches in the tournament?

24. Which city hosted the finals at the 2010 T20 World Cup?

25. Who has the highest batting average in the tournament?

26. How many matches has MS Dhoni played as the captain?
a. 0   b. 19   c. 33   d. 48

27. Which country has scored a victory with a massive 172 runs margin in the tournament?

28. Which two countries have scored a victory by 10 wickets in the T20 World Cup?

BEN STOKES

1. When did Ben Stokes make his England debut?
a. 2009   b. 2010   c. 2011   d. 2012

2. Who was captain when Ben Stokes made his England debut?

3. At which Ashes did Stokes hit his maiden Test century?

4. How many ducks did Stokes score in the home Test series against India in 2014?
a. 0   b. 1   c. 2   d. 3

5. How many scores of 80+ did Stokes hit at the 2019 World Cup?
a. 3   b. 4   c. 5   d. 6

6. How many balls did it take for Stokes to achieve his double century against South Africa in 2016?
a. 163   b. 178   c. 193   d. 207

7. How many T20 half centuries has Stokes achieved?
a. 0   b. 1   c. 6   d. 10

8. Which Big Bash League team did Stokes play for in 2015?

9. When was Stokes born?
a. 1989   b. 1990   c. 1991   d. 1992

10. True or false: Stokes is the highest paid English cricketer in 2021.

11. Against which team did he make his debut?
a. South Africa   b. Australia   c. Pakistan

12. Against which team did he score his career best score in 2015?
a. Ireland   b. South Africa   c. Bangladesh

13. What is Stokes' full name?
a. Benjamin Andrew Stokes
b. Ben Martin Stokes
c. Benjamin Woodrow Stokes

14. In which season did he become the highest paid overseas player in the history of the IPL?
a. 2016   b. 2017   c. 2018   d. 2019

15. What is his highest score in Test cricket?
a. 192   b. 229   c. 258   d. 288

16. As of September 2021, how many centuries has Stokes had in Test cricket?
a. 8   b. 10   c. 12   d. 14

17. Which ICC award did Stokes win in 2019?

18. Ben Stokes has only managed one century in T20. Against which team was it?
a. Mumbai Indians   b. Gujarat Lions
c. Punjab Kings   d. Sunrisers Hyderabad

19. In which country was Stokes born?

20. Does Ben Stokes bat left or right-handed?

INDIA-PAKISTAN RIVALRY

1. In which year was the first India Pakistan match played?
a. 1912   b. 1936   c. 1952   d. 1967

2. Who has scored the highest number of runs in India-Pakistan ODI matches?

3. What is the highest ever ODI score for India against Pakistan?
a. 304   b. 356   c. 417

4. Who won the first India-Pakistan ODI match?

5. Who was the Player of the Series when India defeated Pakistan in the 2004 Test series?

6. Who scored a century while playing in his 100th Test during the India vs Pakistan Test in Bengaluru in 2005?
a. Asif Iqbal
b. Intikhab Alam
c. Inzamam-ul-Haq
d. Asif Masood

7. During the 1999 Chennai Test, in India's second innings, only two batsmen scored greater than 10. One of them was Sachin Tendulkar who scored a century. Who was the other batsman?
a. Anil Kumble
b. Nayan Mongia
c. VVS Laxman
d. Rahul Dravid

8. In the Test series between the two teams in 2007, this Pakistani batsman achieved 464 runs with an average of 116 and also got two centuries.

9. During the Karachi Test between the two teams in 1989, apart from Sachin Tendulkar, who was the other cricketer to make his Test debut for India?
a. Salil Ankola
b. Kapil Dev
c. Ravi Shastri

10. In the 2006 Test series between the two teams, which Pakistan batsman was twice dismissed in the 190s?
a. Younis Khan   b. Danish Kaneria
c. Shoaib Malik   d. Shahid Afridi

11. Which Indian opening pair came close to breaking the then record for the highest opening partnership in an innings in a Test against Pakistan in 2006?

12. How many matches have India and Pakistan played against each other in the Cricket World Cup?
a. 5   b. 7   c. 9   d. 11

13. How many matches have Pakistan won against India in the Cricket World Cup?
a. 0   b. 1   c. 5   d. 6

14. How many matches has Pakistan won against India in the T20 World Cup?
a. 0   b. 1   c. 2   d. 3

15. How many times have Pakistan and India played against each other in a Test match?
a. 41   b. 59   c. 78   d. 102

16. Which country has won 73 out of the total 132 ODI matches played against each other?

17. How many ODI matches has India won against Pakistan?
a. 47   b. 51   c. 55   d. 59

18. How many times has Pakistan won against India out of the total 8 times they faced each other in T20 International?
a. 0   b. 1   c. 3   d. 4

19. What is special about the following cricket players: Abdul Hafeez Kardar, Amir Elahi and Gul Mohammad?

20. What is the highest ever Test score for Pakistan against India?
a. 499   b. 599   c. 699   d. 799

21. Which bowler took the greatest number of wickets in Test matches played between the two countries?

22. What is the highest ever Test score for India against Pakistan?
a. 385   b. 502   c. 675   d. 808

23. What is the highest ever ODI score for Pakistan against India?
a. 344   b. 379   c. 444   d. 482

24. What is the highest number of individual runs scored by a player in an ODI match between the two countries?
a. 108   b. 132   c. 159   d. 194

ENGLAND CRICKET

1. True or false: cricket originated in England.

2. Which England player has the record for the most centuries?

3. Which England player has achieved the second most centuries in Test cricket?

4. Which England cricketer, born in 1848, is known as 'the father of cricket'? He famously advertised mustard at the height of his career.

5. Which England cricket ground was the first to host an English Test match in 1880?

6. How many wickets did Yorkshire-born Wilfred Rhodes take in his impressive career?
a. 1845   b. 3045   c. 4204   d. 5799

7. Stuart Broad's father was also a good cricketer. What is his name?

8. Internationally, which countries do the England team represent?

9. Which county does Joe Root represent?
a. Lancashire   b. Glamorgan   c. Yorkshire

10. In which country was Eoin Morgan born?
a. Germany   b. France   c. Ireland   d. Canada

11. England legend Alec Stewart was born on 8.4.63. How many Test runs did he achieve in his career?

12. True or false: the 2019 World Cup was the first time that England won the World Cup.

13. When were England last ranked number one in Test cricket?
a. 1958   b. 1972   c. 1990   d. 2012

14. How many county cricket teams are there in England and Wales?
a. 12   b. 14   c. 16   d. 18

15. England's longest ever game of cricket happened against South Africa in 1939. How many days did it last?
a. 8   b. 10   c. 12   d. 14

16. After all of that cricket, which team eventually won?

17. True or false: the first cricket World Cup was held in England.

18. In 2021, England lost to India in Ahmedabad in one of the shortest games in history. How many balls were bowled?
a. 288   b. 495   c. 639   d. 842

19. Which county did Ian Botham play for throughout his career?

20. In which year did Moeen Ali make his England cricket debut?
a. 2012   b. 2013   c. 2014   d. 2015

21. Which cricketer served as vice-captain during the 2019 World Cup?

22. Who was the England captain from 1986-1988?

23. In which year was Stuart Broad born?
a. 1980   b. 1983   c. 1986   d. 1989

24. The first ever cricket ball was made in England, but what was it made from?
a. Wool   b. Wood   c. Cow hide

25. What type of wood are most cricket bats in England made from?

26. Wilfred Rhodes is the oldest man to represent England at an international level. How old was he in his last game?
a. 48 years   b. 52 years   c. 56 years

27. How old was Brian Close when he became the youngest person to represent England internationally?

28. When did the England women's team first win the World Cup?
a. 1973 b. 1982 c. 1993 d. 1997

29. True or false: when cricket was first played in England there was only one stump.

30. The 1992 Pakistani cricket captain (and later President) studied at which English university?

31. When did Chris Woakes make his England cricket debut?
a. 2009 b. 2010 c. 2011 d. 2012

32. Which county cricket team did Graham Gooch captain?

33. Where was Andrew Strauss born?

34. Which county cricket club does Dawid Malan play for?

35. In which year did Jofra Archer make his England cricket debut?
a. 2017 b. 2018 c. 2019 d. 2020

MS DHONI

1. Where did MS Dhoni make his Test captaincy debut?

2. Who is MS Dhoni's only ODI wicket?

3. Dhoni's maiden Test and ODI century both came against the same opponent. Name the team.
a. Bangladesh   b. Pakistan   c. West Indies

4. MS Dhoni made a surprise Test retirement call at the age of 33. Where did he play his final Test?
a. Melbourne Cricket Ground   b. The Oval
c. Sydney Cricket Ground   d. Old Trafford

5. Which rank does MS Dhoni hold in the Territorial Indian army which was conferred upon him?

6. MS Dhoni has captained India in 332 international games which is the most out of all cricketers, but under whose captaincy has he played the most?

7. It took MS Dhoni 76 innings before registering his first T20I fifty. Against which team did he finally get it?
 a. Sri Lanka   b. England   c. Pakistan

8. Which of these IPL records does MS Dhoni hold?
a. Most matches b. Most catches
c. Most sixes   d. Most runs in the 20th over

SHANE WARNE

1. True or false: Shane Warne captained Australia in 10 ODI wins.

2. True or false: Shane Warne's highest Test score of 99 is the lowest among those who have played more than 140 Tests.

3. At which ground has Warne taken the most international wickets?
a. Lord's   b. Melbourne Cricket Ground
c. Eden Park   d. Sydney Cricket Ground

4. Shane Warne's final ODI came in which year?
a. 2004   b. 2005   c. 2006   d. 2007

5. Shane Warne's 700th Test wicket was which cricketer?
a. Michael Vaughan   b. Chris Read
c. Andrew Flintoff   d. Andrew Strauss

6. True or false: Shane Warne was the leading wicket-taker across the three World Cups held in the 1990s.

7. True or false: Shane Warne took over 100 wickets in 2005.

8. Which of these batsmen fell to Shane Warne in eight consecutive Test innings against Australia?
a. Vernon Philander   b. Ashwell Prince
c. Robin Peterson   d. Rusty Theron

9. How many wickets has Shane Warne taken in his Test career?
a. 589   b. 708   c. 837   d. 993

DALE STEYN

1. Dale Steyn and which other South African player made their First-Class debuts and their Test debuts in the same match?
a. Boeta Dippennar   b. Jacques Rudolph
c. AB de Villiers   d. Andrew Hall

2. Which batsman has Dale Steyn dismissed the greatest number of times across all formats of international cricket?
a. MS Dhoni   b. Michael Clarke
c. Harbhajan Singh   d. Mohammad Hafeez

3. At which ground was Dale Steyn booed by fans after he decided to shut up shop with the bat and played for a draw when his side needed 16 runs with three wickets in hand against India in 2013?
a. Johannesburg   b. Durban
c. Cape Town   d. Port Elizabeth

4. In which year did Dale Steyn win the ICC Test cricketer of the year?
a. 2002   b. 2004   c. 2006   d. 2008

5. Of the five ten-fers that Dale Steyn has taken in his Test career, two of them have come against the same team in back-to-back Tests. Name the team.
a. India   b. New Zealand
c. West Indies   d. England

6. Which of these South African Test records does not belong to Dale Steyn?
a. Most Wickets
b. Most five-wicket hauls in an innings
c. Most matches by a fast bowler
d. Most ten-wicket hauls in a Test

7. Which is the only IPL team to have kept Dale Steyn across a major auction?
a. Royal Challengers Bangalore
b. Deccan Chargers
c. Sunrisers Hyderabad
d. Gujarat Lions

8. Which of the following Hollywood movies was Dale Steyn a part of?
a. Deadpool   b. Avengers
c. Blended   d. Spider Man

9. "I was furious inside. I was like: 'I am going to get this guy, I have got my eye on you, buddy. I am coming for you.' Every time I play against you, I want you to remember who I am."
True to his promise, Dale Steyn got this batsman out six times in the next six years. Which batsman was he talking about?
a. Ricky Ponting   b. Chris Gayle
c. Michael Clarke   d. Sachin Tendulkar

10. 8.1-6-8-6 - Against which team did Dale Steyn record this iconic spell in a Test?
a. India   b. England
c. New Zealand   d. Pakistan

KEVIN PIETERSEN

1. When was Pietersen born?
a. 1974   b. 1976   c. 1978   d. 1980

2. What is Pietersen's full name?
a. Kevin Kelvin Pieterson
b. Kevin Peter Pieterson
c. Kevin Son Pieterson

3. Pietersen moved to England in 1999, so how is he able to qualify for the England team?
a. Through his mum   b. Through his dad
c. Through his grandfather

4. Pietersen made his England debut in 2004, but against which team was it?
a. Zimbabwe   b. South Africa   c. Australia

5. True or false: Pietersen made his Test debut at the Ashes.

6. Which county cricket club did Pietersen play for?

7. What is Pietersen's highest ever Test score?
a. 227   b. 254   c. 288   d. 301

8. Pietersen took the wickets for the opening three batsmen in his last Test for England. Against which team was he playing?

9. How many Test centuries did Pietersen achieve in his career?
a. 19   b. 23   c. 27   d. 31

10. In which year did Pietersen become captain?
a. 2006   b. 2007   c. 2008   d. 2009

MISCELLANEOUS

1. Which country co-hosted the 1987 World Cup with India?

2. Which team finished runners-up at the 2015 World Cup?

3. Who was England's head coach for the 2019 World Cup?

4. What is the width of a cricket pitch?
a. 2m   b. 3m   c. 4m   d. 5m

5. What colour is an ODI cricket ball?

6. What is the length of a cricket pitch?
a. 12m   b. 15m   c. 18m   d. 20m

7. What does ODI stand for?

8. How many people watched the 2015 World Cup worldwide?
a. 500 million   b. 1 billion   c. 1.5 billion

9. How many times have Australia won the World Cup?
a. 3   b. 4   c. 5   d. 6

10. Which player has taken the most ODI wickets?

11. Which player scored the most runs in the 2015 World Cup?

12. What piece of protective equipment is worn on a player's legs?

13. Where does the Kookaburra cricket bat originate from?

14. Which player holds the record for the fastest hundred in an ODI?

15. Who captained India in the 2015 World Cup final?

16. Which year was the World Cup held in the West Indies?

17. Which ODI bowler was the fastest to take 100 wickets?

18. Which team does Mark Wood represent?

19. What is a ball that bounces over your shoulder called?

20. Which 2 teams played the first game of cricket?

21. When was the first official match ever held?
a. 1877   b. 1890   c. 1910   d. 1856

22. Following an incident on the field, the umpire repeatedly taps his left shoulder with his right hand. What is the umpire trying to signal here?

23. What is the maximum number of overs a bowler can bowl in T-20 cricket?

24. How many substitutes can each team have in Test cricket?
a. 4   b. 5   c. 6   d. 7

25. What does the term LBW stand for in cricket?

26. What does the term power play mean in cricket?

27. What is the maximum number of overs a bowler can bowl in a 50 over ODI game?
a. 5   b. 7   c. 8   d. 10

28. A maximum of five fielders only are allowed on the leg-side by the fielding side at once in limited overs internationals. What is the maximum number of fielders allowed on the off-side at any time?
a. 8   b. 9   c. 10   d. 11

29. Which of these is not a way of getting out?
a. Running on the pitch   b. Timed out
c. Obstructing the field   d. Handling the ball

30. As per the MCC Laws, What is the total number of ways in which a player can be out in a game of cricket?
a. 5   b. 8   c. 10   d. 15

31. What does the term "to bowl a maiden over" mean?
a. Knock a lady over
b. An over where no runs are scored
c. Bowl the first over of a match
d. None of the above

32. Harold ("Dickie") Bird is best known for his career in cricket as what?

33. In which year were the first laws of cricket believed to have been written?
a. 1640   b. 1682   c. 1743   d. 1774

34. What is the slang word given to a ball that is bowled so well that the batsman is unable to play it?

35. What does it mean if an umpire raises both arms straight above his head?

36. True or False: Lord's got its name because of how popular the game was with the English aristocracy.

37. True or False: The Wisden Cricketers' Almanack has information and statistics about all aspects of cricket from every year, which is why it is also known as the 'bible of cricket'.

38. True or False: A score of 111 is known as a "Nelson."

39. What is the nickname of Zimbabwe's national men's cricket team?

40. What is the term given to a score of zero by a batsman?

41. True or False: Australian cricketer Sir Donald Bradman ended his career with a batting average of 99.94 runs in International matches.

42. Which of the following bowlers has the fastest recorded bowling speed of all time?
a. Brett Lee   b. Shaun Tait
c. Shoaib Akhtar   d. Jeff Thomson

43. Queensland's premier cricket ground is known as what?

44. Big Bird, Super Cat and Whispering Death are nicknames for players from which country?

45. True or False: A cricket Test match can end in a draw even if one team has scored a greater number of runs than the other.

46. Which country has a fanatical supporter's group called the "Barmy Army"?

47. What are extras in cricket?

48. What is a bye in cricket?

49. Another new concept of T-20 cricket is the free hit, wherein a batsman gets a chance to have a free hit at the ball knowing that he cannot be given out. When does the free hit come into play?

50. How many overs of powerplay are allowed?

51. True or false: a bowler bowls a beamer at the batsman which misses his head. This is then called a no-ball by the umpire. The batsman gets a free hit on the next delivery.

52. How long is the duration of one innings of a T-20 match?

53. In T-20 cricket, how many bouncers are allowed in any over?

54. How many drink breaks are allowed in a T-20 innings?

55. Why do batsmen in T-20 matches sit near to the boundary, rather than sitting in the dressing room?

56. The umpire "offers the light" to the batting side. What does this mean?

57. When the umpire puts both arms across each other in front of his stomach, it means what?

58. What is the maximum number of overs a bowler can bowl in T-20 cricket?

59. What happens if the bowler accidently throws the ball backwards as they approach the crease?

60. What would happen if a fielder caught the ball with their cap?

61. What happens if the ball strikes a close fielder on their helmet before being caught?

ANSWERS

WORLD CUP/ ODI WORLD CUP

1. 1975
2. England
3. West Indies
4. Every 4 years
5. Australia
6. Sachin Tendulkar
7. Glenn McGrath
8. England
9. James Faulkner
10. Aravinda De Silva
11. West Indies
12. India
13. 1983
14. Madan Lal
15. Javagal Srinath
16. Eoin Morgan
17. Munaf Patel-Sreesanth
18. 125 runs
19. 275 runs
20. 1983
21. 1983
22. 1992
23. Kane Williamson
24. MS Dhoni
25. Ben Stokes
26. 237
27. Sachin Tendulkar
28. Mitchell Starc
29. Ricky Ponting
30. Kumar Sangakkara
31. 1987
32. Chris Gayle and Kevin Samuels
33. 318 runs
34. 7
35. 8 wickets

36. 1743 runs
37. 215 runs
38. Rahul Dravid
39. Geoff Allott and Shane Warne
40. Sachin Tendulkar
41. Anil Kumble
42. South Africa
43. Ricky Ponting
44. Clive Lloyd
45. London
46. K.J.J.Van Noortwijk
47. Glen Turner
48. 17
49. Zimbabwe
50. Bangladesh

ICC WORLD TEST CHAMPIONSHIP

1. Joe Root
2. Ravi Chandran Ashwin
3. Lasith Embuldeniya
4. JC Butler
5. Kane Williamson and Henry Nicholls
6. Stuart Broad
7. Quinton de Kock
8. JE Root
9. KA Jamieson
10. New Zealand
11. 335 runs
12. 254 runs
13. 1152 runs
14. Rohit Sharma and Ben Stokes
15. JE Root
16. 24
17. India

IPL

1. Virat Kohli
2. 166 wickets
3. MS Dhoni
4. 144
5. S Ravi
6. Rohit Sharma
7. SL Malinga
8. 223 Runs
9. One
10. 2012
11. 2013
12. Gautam Gambhir
13. SP Narine
14. Harbhajan Singh
15. He went unsold
16. Yusuf Pathan
17. Kochi Tuskers Kerala and Pune Warriors India
18. Steve Smith
19. James Hopes
20. M. Chinnaswamy Stadium, Bengaluru
21. James Faulkner
22. KL Rahul
23. David Warner
24. Chris Gayle
25. Kagiso Rabada
26. Mumbai Indians
27. Glenn Maxwell
28. 8
29. $4.1 Billion
30. Bangalore
31. South Africa
32. Deccan Chargers
33. Kolkata Knight Riders
34. 2008
35. 16
36. 14
37. 2
38. Lasith Malinga

39. MS Dhoni
40. Chennai Super Kings
41. Adam Gilchrist
42. Kolkata
43. Brendon McCullum
44. Virat Kohli
45. False- they have never played
46. Laxmipathy Balaji
47. 2
48. 3
49. Shaun Marsh
50. Sohail Tanvir
51. Manish Pandey
52. Rohit Sharma
53. Bangalore
54. Bangalore
55. Shane Warne
56. Chennai Super Kings
57. Stephen Fleming
58. Delhi Dare Devils
59. Rohit Sharma
60. 175
61. 2010
62. Dwayne Bravo
63. Suresh Raina
64. Kumar Sangakkara
65. 1
66. Lasith Malinga
67. 2
68. Praveen Kumar
69. Suresh Raina
70. Dinesh Karthik
71. 73
72. Virat Kohli
73. Hyderabad
74. Harbhajan Singh
75. Virat Kohli

SACHIN TENDULKAR

1. Sri Lanka
2. South Africa
3. Kochi
4. Roshan Mahanama
5. Kapil Dev
6. Inzamam-ul-Haq
7. Zimbabwe
8. Justin Kemp
9. Shahid Afridi
10. Umar Gul
11. South Africa
12. Anderson Cummins
13. 1
14. 2009
15. Allan Lamb

THE ASHES

1. England and Australia
2. Test Cricket
3. 1882
4. 5
5. 71
6. 33
7. 32
8. 6
9. Sir Donald Bradman
10. Shane Warne
11. 579
12. 332
13. 1868
14. 2
15. 66th
16. 1998
17. 2013
18. Ben Stokes
19. Michael Slater
20. Shane Watson
21. Ashton Agar
22. 7
23. Steve Waugh
24. Marcus North
25. 23
26. 8
27. William Bates
28. Billy Midwinter
29. Sammy Woods
30. Jason Gillespie
31. Marcus Trescothick
32. 22
33. George McShane
34. Nathan Lyon
35. 8
36. The Invincibles
37. Australia
38. True

39. Mark Taylor
40. Terry Alderman
41. 2
42. Trevor Hohns
43. Robin Smith
44. David Gower
45. Greg Campbell
46. Australia-England 4-0
47. Australia won both by 45 runs
48. C Bannerman
49. Ian Botham
50. A Lock
51. Bradman's 1948 team
52. Trent Bridge, Nottingham
53. The Bodyline Series
54. Shane Warne
55. Thomson & Lillee
56. Jim Laker
57. Substitute Fieldsman
58. David Hookes
59. Ashton Agar
60. Leg Spinner

ICC CHAMPIONS TROPHY

1. 1998
2. Bangladesh
3. One Day International
4. South Africa
5. 2
6. Australia and India
7. India
8. Kenya
9. Chris Gayle
10. Kyle Mills
11. Pakistan
12. Sri Lanka and India
13. 2
14. India and West Indies
15. 2025
16. New Zealand
17. West Indies and South Africa
18. India
19. Kenya
20. Bangladesh
21. Marcus Trescothick
22. USA
23. New Zealand
24. Mohammad Amir
25. India
26. Josh Hazlewood
27. Shoaib Malik
28. Imad Wasim

ICC T20 WORLD CUP

1. 2007
2. Mahela Jayawardene
3. Shahid Afridi
4. South Africa
5. India and Pakistan
6. 1
7. West Indies
8. India
9. West Indies
10. Sri Lanka
11. 2021
12. Adam Gilchrist
13. Andrew Flintoff
14. Umar Gul
15. Hershelle Gibbs
16. Craig McMillan
17. Mark Gillespie
18. Chris Gayle
19. BAW Mendis
20. 123 Runs
21. 117 Runs
22. Ab De Villiers
23. TM Dilshan
24. London
25. Virat Kohli
26. 33 Matches
27. Sri Lanka
28. Australia and South Africa

BEN STOKES

1. 2011
2. Eoin Morgan
3. 2013/14 Ashes
4. 3
5. 4
6. 163
7. 0
8. The Melbourne Renegades
9. 1991
10. True
11. Australia
12. South Africa
13. Benjamin Andrew Stokes
14. 2017
15. 258
16. 10
17. ICC Player of the Year
18. Gujarat Lions
19. New Zealand
20. Left-handed

INDIA-PAKISTAN RIVALRY

1. 1952
2. Sachin Tendulkar
3. 356
4. Pakistan
5. Virender Shehwag
6. Inzamam-ul-Haq
7. Nayan Mongia
8. Misbah-ul-Haq
9. Salil Ankola
10. Younis Khan
11. Virender Sehwag, Rahul Dravid
12. 7
13. 0
14. 0
15. 59
16. Pakistan
17. 55
18. 1
19. They have all competed for both Pakistan and India
20. 699
21. Kapil Dev(99)
22. 675
23. 344
24. 194

ENGLAND CRICKET

1. True
2. Alastair Cook
3. Kevin Pietersen
4. W.G. Grace
5. The Oval
6. 4204
7. Chris Broad
8. England and Wales
9. Yorkshire
10. Ireland
11. 8463
12. True
13. 1958
14. 18
15. 14
16. It was a draw because the ship was waiting to take England home
17. True
18. 842
19. Somerset
20. 2014
21. Jos Buttler
22. Mike Gatting
23. 1986
24. Wool
25. Willow
26. 52 years
27. 18 years old
28. 1973
29. False - it started with 2 stumps
30. Oxford
31. 2011
32. Essex
33. South Africa
34. Yorkshire
35. 2019

MSD

1. Kanpur
2. Travis Dowlin
3. Pakistan
4. MCG, Melbourne
5. Lieutenant Colonel
6. Rahul Dravid
7. England
8. Most runs in the 20th over

SHANE WARNE

1. True
2. False
3. Sydney Cricket Ground
4. 2005
5. Andrew Strauss
6. False
7. False
8. Ashwell Prince
9. 708

DALE STEYN

1. AB de Villiers
2. Mohammad Hafeez
3. Johannesburg
4. 2008
5. New Zealand
6. Most matches by a fast bowler
7. Sunrisers Hyderabad
8. Blended
9. Ricky Ponting
10. Pakistan

KEVIN PIETERSON

1. 1980
2. Kevin Peter Pieterson
3. Through his mum
4. Zimbabwe
5. True
6. Surrey
7. 227
8. South Africa
9. 23
10. 2008

MISCELLANEOUS

1. Pakistan
2. New Zealand
3. Trevor Bayliss
4. 3m
5. White
6. 20m
7. One Day International
8. 1.5 billion
9. 5
10. Muttiah Muralitharan
11. Martin Guptill
12. Batting Pads
13. Australia
14. Ab De Villiers
15. MS Dhoni
16. 2007
17. Rashid Khan
18. England
19. Bouncer
20. England and Australia
21. 1877
22. Penalty for the batting side
23. 4
24. 6
25. Leg Before Wicket
26. Restrictions on the placement of fielders
27. 10
28. 9
29. Running on the pitch
30. 10
31. An over where no runs are scored
32. An umpire
33. 1774
34. A jaffa

35. The batsman has scored six runs
36. False
37. True
38. True
39. The Chevrons
40. A duck
41. True
42. Shoaib Akhtar
43. The Gabba
44. West Indies
45. True
46. England
47. Runs that are not scored off the bat
48. A run scored when the keeper fails to stop the ball
49. When the bowler bowls a no ball
50. 6
51. False
52. 75 minutes
53. 1
54. 0
55. To reach the field of play quickly
56. Asking whether they want to play on if the light is poor
57. Signalling a dead ball
58. 4
59. The ball is considered dead
60. The batsman receives five runs
61. The batsman is not out

Printed in Great Britain
by Amazon

11036271R00056